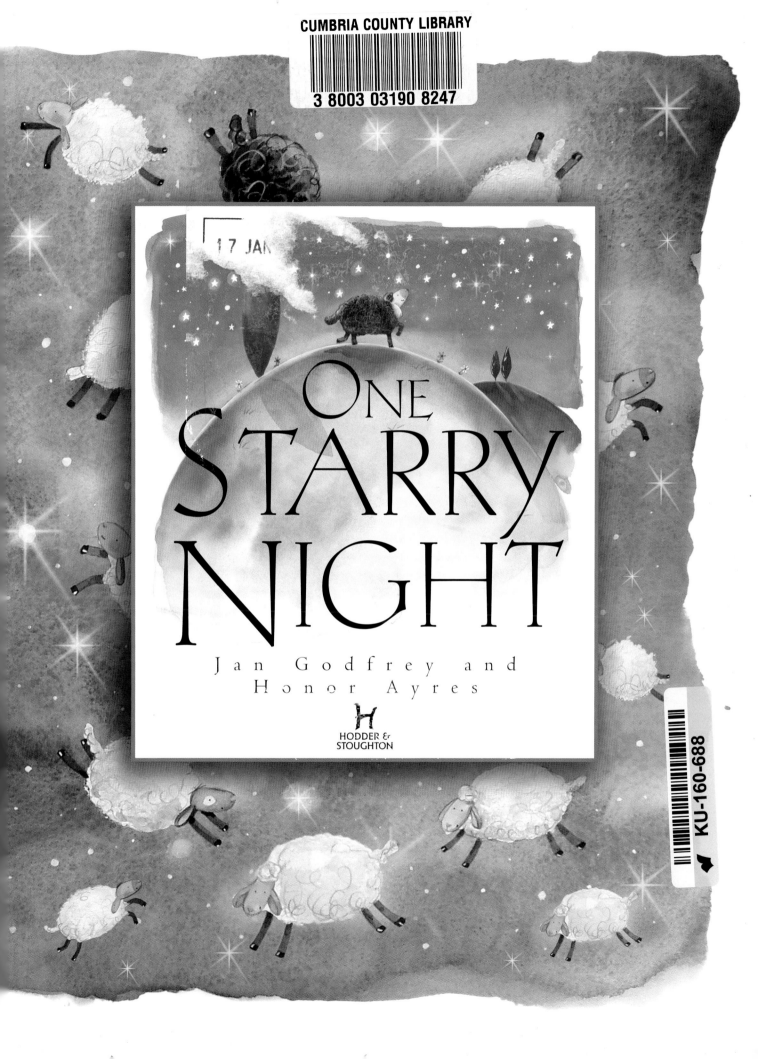

1 7 JAN

ONE STARRY NIGHT

Jan Godfrey and
Honor Ayres

H

HODDER &
STOUGHTON

One starry night, a shepherd boy came over a hill near Bethlehem.

Behind him came one little sheep, half-asleep.

Baa

said the one little sheep.

Another little sheep came ambling over the hill, yawning. Now there were two little sheep with the shepherd boy, half-asleep and yawning.

Baa

Baa

said the two little sheep.

Another little sheep came over the hill, weary.
Now there were three little sheep with the shepherd boy,
half-asleep and yawning and weary.

Baa   Baa Baa

said the three little sheep.

Another little sheep came over the hill, wandering about.
Now there were four little sheep with the shepherd boy,
half-asleep and yawning and weary and wandering.

Baa **Baa** **Baa** **Baa**

said the four little sheep.

7

Another little sheep came over the hill, slipping on the stones. Now there were five little sheep with the shepherd boy, half-asleep and yawning and weary and wandering and slipping.

Baa Baa **Baa** Baa **Baa**

said the five little sheep.

Another little sheep came over the hill, sliding here and there.
Now there were six little sheep with the shepherd boy,
half-asleep and yawning and weary and wandering
and slipping and sliding.

Baa   Baa   Baa   Baa   Baa   Baa

said the six little sheep.

Another little sheep came over the hill, stumbling on the path. Now there were seven little sheep with the shepherd boy, half-asleep and yawning and weary and wandering and slipping and sliding and stumbling.

Baa Baa **Baa** Baa Baa Baa Baa

said the seven little sheep.

Another little sheep came over the hill, tripping over a rock. Now there were eight little sheep with the shepherd boy, half-asleep and yawning and weary and wandering and slipping and sliding and stumbling and tripping.

Baa **Baa** **Baa** **Baa** **Baa** **Baa**
said the eight little sheep. **Baa** **Baa**

Another little sheep came over the hill, trotting along.
Now there were nine little sheep with the shepherd boy,
half-asleep and yawning and weary and wandering and slipping
and sliding and stumbling and tripping and trotting.

Baa
Baa Baa
Baa
Baa
Baa
Baa Baa
Baa

said the nine little sheep.

Another little sheep came over the hill, grumpy.
   Now there were ten little sheep with the shepherd boy,
half-asleep and yawning and weary and wandering and slipping
and sliding and stumbling and tripping and trotting and grumpy.

Baa   Baa   Baa   **Baa**

Baa   **Baa**   Baa   Baa   Baa

Baa

said the ten little sheep.

They huddled together with the shepherd boy,
and started to fall asleep...

And then – it happened!

A glorious angel appeared, and the sheep were very afraid.

Baa   Baa   Baa   Baa   Baa

Baa   Baa

Baa

Baa   Baa

said the ten little sheep.

'Whaaaaat?'
said the shepherd boy, who was very afraid too.
  He was so afraid that he shivered and shook,
and his mouth stayed open for quite a few minutes
in a big, round 'O'.

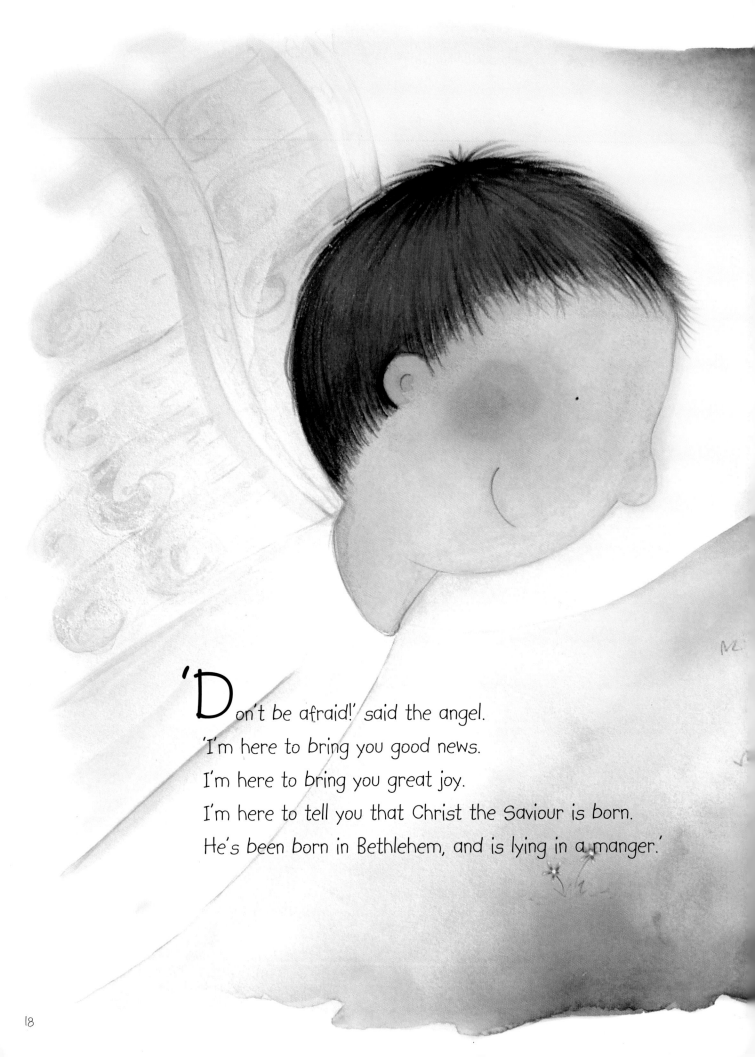

'Don't be afraid!' said the angel.
'I'm here to bring you good news.
I'm here to bring you great joy.
I'm here to tell you that Christ the Saviour is born.
He's been born in Bethlehem, and is lying in a manger.'

Then the starry sky was filled with light,
and the sound of angels singing.
'Glory to God', sang the angels.

'Glory to God in the highest.
Glory to God in the highest and peace on earth,
Peace on earth to everyone!'

The shepherd boy jumped up,
and the ten little sheep jumped up
to follow him.
   Then the one little, two little, three little,
four little, five little, six little, seven little,
eight little, nine little, ten little sheep...

... ran and skipped and gambolled and wriggled and jiggled and jumped and hurried and scurried and scampered and frolicked – all the way down the hill to Bethlehem.

And, with Mary, his mother, and Joseph there too,
they found – just as the angels had promised – a baby!
A baby, lying in a manger;

a baby, lying in a manger in a *stable*;
a baby, lying in a manger in a *stable* in Bethlehem.

Then the shepherd boy
and the ten little sheep worshipped the baby,

because they knew he was Jesus, the son of God.

Dawn came, rosy pink, into a silent world, on that first Christmas morning.

The angels and the stars had disappeared into the sky.

The shepherd boy and the one little, two little, three little, four little, five little, six little, seven little, eight little, nine little, ten little sheep, went running over the hills and far away, to tell the whole world that Jesus, the Saviour of the world, had been born.

Baa

Baa

Baa

Baa

Baa

Baa

Baa

Baa

Baa

Baa

said the ten little sheep.

'Happy Christmas, everyone!'

Published in Great Britain by Hodder & Stoughton,
a division of Hodder Headline Ltd, London NW2 3BH
ISBN 0 340 90949 8

First edition 2006

Copyright © 2006 Anno Domini Publishing,
1 Churchgates, The Wilderness, Berkhamsted, Herts HP4 2UB, UK
Text copyright © 2006 Jan Godfrey
Illustrations copyright © 2006 Honor Ayres

Editorial Director Annette Reynolds
Editor Nicola Bull
Art Director Gerald Rogers
Pre-production Krystyna Kowalska Hewitt
Production John Laister

Bristish Library Cataloguing in Publication Data
A record of this book is available from the British Library